seventeen

presents...

500

BEAUTY TIPS

Look Your Best for
School, Weekend, Parties & More!

Library of Congress Cataloging-in-Publication Data

Kristen Oldham
  Seventeen presents--500 beauty tips : look your best for school, weekend, parties & more! / Kristen Oldham.
        p. cm.
    Includes bibliographical references and index.
    ISBN: 978-1-58816-642-5 (alk. paper)
  1. Teenage girls--Health and hygiene--Juvenile literature. 2. Beauty, Personal--Juvenile literature. 3. Cosmetics--Juvenile literature. I. Title. II. Title: 500 beauty tips. III. Title: Five hundred beauty tips.
    RA777.25.F38 2008
    646.7'046—dc22
2007034031
10 9 8 7 6 5 4 3 2 1

YA

Published by Hearst Books
A Division of Sterling Publishing Co., Inc.
387 Park Avenue South, New York, NY 10016

Seventeen is a registered trademark of
Hearst Communications, Inc.

www.seventeen.com

For information about custom editions, special sales, premium and corporate purchases, please contact Sterling Special Sales Department at 800-805-5489 or specialsales@sterlingpublishing.com.

Distributed in Canada by Sterling Publishing
c/o Canadian Manda Group, 165 Dufferin Street
Toronto, Ontario, Canada M6K 3H6

Distributed in Australia by Capricorn Link (Australia) Pty. Ltd.
P.O. Box 704, Windsor, NSW 2756 Australia
Manufactured in China

Sterling ISBN 978-1-58816-642-5

12/24/2009

School

Weekend

Party

Date

Work

Pool

seventeen presents...

500
BEAUTY TIPS

Look Your Best for
School, Weekend, Parties & More!

HEARST BOOKS
A division of Sterling Publishing Co., Inc.

New York / London
www.sterlingpublishing.com

contents

foreword

HEY!

No more stressing in front of the mirror, debating a new look! Consider us your personal stylists. This helpful book is jam-packed with easy makeup ideas and quick beauty tips—so you're sure to make a great impression at any event.

—the editors of *seventeen*

school

Whether you have five minutes or a full hour to get ready, the tricks in this section will help you look pulled-together and pretty—without totally distracting you (and the guys!) from your work.

17 TIP
Stick to classic hair and makeup looks that will last all day and show off your natural beauty and style.

#1

Smell good all day by spraying

PERFUME

at the nape of your neck. The fine hairs that gather here will absorb and hold fragrance longer than skin does.

#2

Play up your

NATURAL GLOW

with a dab of subtle rosy color on your lips, eyelids, and apples of your cheeks.

#3

"Go with an

AEROSOL HAIRSPRAY

to keep hair in place. But hold the can 8 to 10 inches away—any closer and you'll *wet* your hair, which will ruin the style."

– Ken Paves, celebrity hair stylist

#4

Use a

SHIMMERY GLOSS

**to make your lips look fuller,
or a matte lipstick
to make them seem thinner.**

#5

Sprinkle

TALCUM POWDER

on your brush to style your hair
when it's greasy and you don't
have time to wash it.

#6

FRECKLES

are something to highlight, not cover up! Avoid heavy, opaque foundations and powders. Instead, use a tinted moisturizer so everyone can see your complexion.

#7

If you like to style your
hair in the morning,
wash it a half hour

BEFORE BED

and let it dry while you sleep.
Starting with dry hair in the
A.M. will cut styling
time in half.

#8

Save ribbons from gift boxes and bags— they make perfect (and free!) pony accessories and give your look a

SWEET FEEL.

#9

Pinch your cheeks, then

MATCH A BLUSH

to your flushed skin. Blend that color onto your apples to look healthy and cheerful (even when you're not).

#10

Chug at least eight cups of

H_2O

a day. It's been said that staying hydrated can keep your complexion clear.

#11

Carry a small

NAIL FILE

in your bag so
that when you chip
a nail, you can
easily file it instead
of tearing off
the broken piece.

#12

It may seem too much for every day, but matching red lips and rosy cheeks is

CLASSIC.

#13

Try a new style without losing your length by cutting long, side-swept

BANGS.

#14

Try a few

RED LIPCOLORS

to find your perfect match. Start
with a pinky red on fair to beige skin
and brick on golden to deep skin.

#15

Make a hairstyle last—
seal just-spritzed
hairspray with a

BLAST OF COOL AIR

from your blow-dryer.

SpecialEyes
EYE LINER PENCIL

#16

Choose pencil eyeliner instead of liquid. When it smudges after a long day, it will create a cool,

SMOKY-EYE EFFECT.

#17

MINIMIZE FLYAWAYS
by applying a smoothing cream to hair immediately after blowdrying.

great for oily skin

NEW

Clean & Clear®

Morning Burst.

Oil Absorbing SHEETS

Instantly removes excess oil
Won't smudge makeup
Invigorating fragrance

50 SHEETS
Each Sheet Size: 1.9 x 3.1 in. (5 x 8 cm)

Johnson & Johnson

#18

Carry face-blotting

PAPERS

to soak up daytime
oil without smudging
your makeup.

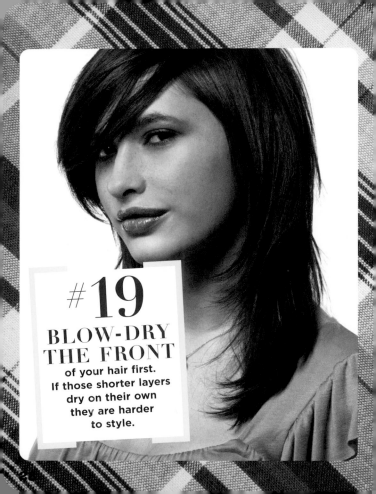

#19

BLOW-DRY THE FRONT

of your hair first.
If those shorter layers
dry on their own
they are harder
to style.

#20

On a bad hair day,
tie a chic

DESIGNER
SCARF

around your hair.
Celebs use this trick
all the time!

#21

For a

SOFT WASH OF COLOR,

apply neutral shimmer all over your lids, then brush blue or violet shadow up to your mid-lid.

#22

A balanced diet will make a big difference in your complexion. That means eating nutrient-rich

GREEN VEGGIES

every day.

#23

Never try to change the
shape of your

NATURAL
BROW ARCH

with tweezing—its highest
point should be right above
the outside of your iris.

#24

DON'T PICK

a zit!
Use a salicylic acid treatment overnight instead.

Clean & Clear®

Advantage®

ACNE SPOT TREATMENT
SALICYLIC ACID ACNE MEDICATION

100% of people showed clearer skin in just one day

Won't overdry skin

Johnson&Johnson

0.75 FL. OZ. (22 mL)

#25

To make your style

LAST ALL DAY

try not to touch it—grease from your palms can weigh it down.

#26

A cool, shimmery pink
cream blush gives
all skin tones a healthy

PUNCH
OF COLOR

and shine.

#27

"If you use depuffing eye creams, make sure they're left on for at least 10 minutes to really

SEE RESULTS."

– Nick Barose, celebrity makeup artist

#28

UPDATE YOUR LOOK
by getting bangs!

#29

AVOID OVERSCRUBBING

your face—it can actually dry out skin
and lead to excess oil.

Schwarzkopf

Zero Frizz

100% RESCUE

CORRECTIVE HAIR SERUM

extra strength
abrillantador correctivo

correct, smooth
tame frizz

[instant frizz relief]

118 ml ℮ 4 FL OZ

#30

"The biggest complaint
I hear is frizz.
My tip? Use a

SILICONE SERUM

on *wet* hair."
– Ken Paves,
celebrity hair stylist

#31

Shorter hair looks
best when it's a
bit dirty and

PIECEY,

so shampoo
every three days
(but still condition
it daily).

#32

Use a
wide-toothed comb

IN THE
SHOWER
to distribute
conditioner evenly.

#33

Store a

TOUCH-UP BEAUTY KIT

in your locker. If
you rushed to school,
you can apply gloss—
or any other steps
you missed—once
you get there.

#34

It can take several weeks for a skin routine to show results—

HANG IN THERE!

#35

HANDS OFF!
Fingers can spread bacteria to your face, making breakouts worse.

#36

Switch to a natural bristle brush.

BOAR BRISTLES
are gentler than metal bristles, which can break hair and cause split ends.

#37

Metal nail files are

TOO HARSH

and can weaken nails.
Choose a gentle
emery board instead.

#38

Whenever you shampoo, you should

ALWAYS CONDITION—

the combo makes all hair types healthier, more manageable, and better-looking.

#**40**

Try a

TOURMALINE HAIR DRYER

if you wash and dry your hair before rushing to school: The ion charge dries hair twice as fast.

#41

VIBRANT PINK

lipstick wakes up
pale skin so much
you can skip the blush.

great for fair skin!

great for ~~fine~~ hair!

#42

Lightly spritz a firm-hold
hairspray all over your
hair to help your

VOLUME

last all day long.

great for dry skin!

#43

Spray water onto your face

BEFORE YOU APPLY CREAM.

Your moisturizer will absorb faster.

#44

Keep natural

CURLS BOUNCY

by rinsing every other day with water; using shampoo only a couple times a week to avoid drying out your curls.

#45

Dark winged liner and almost-black nails make an edgy,

DRAMATIC STATEMENT.

great for the hair!

#46
DON'T ADD WEIGHT
to fine hair—avoid products with alcohol (they flatten thin hair).

great for oily skin →

#47

After exfoliating, rinse your face with warm water, then splash with cold water to

CLOSE PORES

and prevent greasiness.

#48

AVOID
wearing tight-fitting backpacks or sports bras. The friction and sweat can cause body breakouts.

#49

MASSAGE YOUR SCALP

for three minutes to increase blood flow—some say it'll make hair grow faster!

#50

After pulling an

ALL-NIGHTER,

dust your cheekbones with a
warm berry-toned blush to give
your skin a healthy glow.

#51
Always twirling hair? Stop now to
AVOID SPLIT ENDS.

#52

STRENGTHEN

your strands by eating sulfur-
rich foods like milk, fish, eggs.

#53

When showering, don't forget to

LOOFAH YOUR BACK!

Exfoliation is key to remaining acne-free!

#54

Apply a bold, shiny lip color to draw attention to your face. You'll instantly

APPEAR CONFIDENT!

#55

CURE

a *mildly* itchy scalp by applying
conditioner to dry roots.
Let it soak into your scalp
then style as usual.

#56

You know you should drink eight glasses of water a day to keep skin hydrated—but it

HELPS YOUR HAIR TOO

(hair is made of the same proteins as skin).

#57

Apply pink blush to the
apples of your cheeks

AFTER APPLYING
BRONZER—
it will keep your bronzer
from looking muddy.

#58

To avoid greasy
locks, don't use

SILICONE
PRODUCTS
on dry hair.

#59

To

KEEP GLOSS ON LONGER,

line lips with
a nude lipliner
before applying.

#60

For an even distribution, rub products onto your

HANDS FIRST

(like lotion) and then apply to your hair.

#61

To minimize frizz, run

COOL WATER

on your wrists if you
feel hot—hair frizzes
when your body and
scalp temperatures rise.

#62

Keep curls frizz-free—
DON'T TOUCH
your hair as you diffuse it.

great for <u>curly</u> hair

#63

Pair a chic headband
with a messy bun
for a casual, but cute

DAYTIME
STYLE.

great for
dry skin?!

#64

WASH YOUR FACE

with cool or
lukewarm water;
it's less drying
than hot.

#65

"PASTELS
are a great way to wear color on
your eyes in a subtle, everyday way."
– Tamah Krinsky, NYC makeup artist

#66

AVOID WEIGHING DOWN HAIR

by applying conditioner from mid-hair shaft to ends—skip your roots.

great for ~~fine~~ hair!

#67

If the ends of your hair are fried,

SHAMPOO JUST YOUR ROOTS

every other day.

#68

Curl the ends of a

BASIC PONYTAIL

to make it more polished and fun.

#69
PREVENT
dull, splotchy skin
by getting at
least seven hours
of sleep a night.

#70

Sweep

COLORFUL SHADOWS

across just your lids—not to your browbones—for a more subdued look.

#71

To shrink lumpy, cystic acne

APPLY A DAB

of hydrocortisone cream twice daily.

#72

Instead of using a rubber band
or pencil to keep hair off your
face during study sessions,

USE HAIRPINS

with plastic-covered tips.
They won't damage locks.

#73

Start taking a multivitamin with

FOLIC ACID

everyday. It helps maintain healthy hair.

#74

To make bright eyeliner

WEARABLE

for day, line your bottom or
top lid—not both.

#75

Retire your basic
ponytail for a

PRETTY
CHIGNON
to keep hair off
your face during class.

SOOTHING · COOLING · REFRESHING

BURT'S BEES

BEESWAX LIP BALM

Carrot

Yes TO carrots™

C Me Smile
Lip Butter

95% Organic · All-natural

Neutrogena®
Lip Moisturizer

with PABA-free sunblock protection

76

Dab on

LIP BALM

before applying dark
lipstick to moisten lips so
they won't get flaky.

#77

Curly haired girls should apply product right out of the shower while hair is soaking wet for the

PRETTIEST CURLS.

great for curly hair

#78

A dirty cell phone
can cause acne.
Wipe it daily with

ASTRINGENT.

#79

**A low pony
is simple but still**

GLAM.

#80

Pat

DON'T RUB!

skin dry with a towel
so you won't irritate it.

#81

Love a

STRONG STATEMENT?

Try two different bright liners—one in top, one on bottom.

#82

Apply an antiperspirant that

LASTS 24 HOURS

before bed—that way if you oversleep and can't shower, you're covered.

#83

Dab a bright

RED LIPGLOSS

in the center of your lips
and smooth outward—the
shine will make your lips
look full and kissable.

#84

If you need to

REFRESH YOUR MASCARA,

comb through your lashes first then apply a second coat so it doesn't get clumpy.

#85

Prone to grease?

PREVENT OILY ROOTS

by brushing only twice a day; overbrushing stimulates the scalp to produce more oil.

#86

Keep your hairstyle classic for

SCHOOL PHOTOS:

try a simple blow-dry with a slightly off-center part. You'll regret anything super-trendy in a few years.

weekend

Weekends are your days off from the usual routine, so use these tips to spend less time styling your hair and doing your makeup (a little blush can go a long way), and more time treating yourself with a deep conditioner or an at home spa treatment.

17 TIP
Go for minimal hair and makeup. A little foundation and gloss will keep you covered.

#87

"If your hair is layered, it will make it much easier to create a

BEACHY TEXTURE."

– Creighton, celebrity hair stylist

H_2O

#88

Keep your hair soft
year-round by applying

LEAVE-IN
CONDITIONER

before you go outside to
protect your locks.

#89

To make cream shadow
last, glide on in

THIN
LAYERS,
letting each dry
before adding more.

PANTENE
style PRO-V

NEW

ICE SHINE
hairspray
all-day hold and
gorgeous shine

maximum hold
control máximo

NET WT/PESO NETO 234 g (8.25 OZ)

#90
For a beachy texture,
SPRITZ
DAMP
HAIR
with hairspray and
sleep on it. Tossing
in bed crumples
your hair to make
pretty bends.

#91

Make long-lasting lip color
look more like a stain by

USING YOUR FINGER

to apply the product.

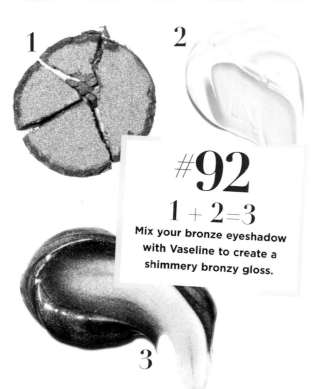

1

2

#92

1 + 2 = 3

Mix your bronze eyeshadow
with Vaseline to create a
shimmery bronzy gloss.

3

#93

Make your products
MULTITASK—
use a cream bronzer on
eyes, cheeks, *and* lips.

#94

Get soft strands—
in place of styling products, use
CONDITIONER.

#95

Smooth a tinted moisturizer with SPF all over your face to give yourself a little bit of

GLOWY COLOR

plus protection from the sun.

#96

A touch of

PINK BLUSH

on your cheeks will make your
skin look alive even if you
don't wear anything else.

#97

LIVEN UP HAIR
without much work by using
leave-in conditioner, then
lightly scrunching hair.

skin effects
by Dr. Jeffrey Dover

Sun Effects

SPF **45**
Sunscreen Lotion

with
Dermaplex™
Technology

6 FL OZ (177 mL)

#98

MIX SUNBLOCK

with your tinted moisturizer in your hand then apply all over your face—it will protect your skin *and* keep imperfections covered all day.

#99

If your scalp is

SENSITIVE,

wait a day after
washing to dye
your hair.

great for straight hair!

#100

Get loose waves—
pull damp hair
up into a high,

LOOSE BUN.

When it's dry,
undo the elastic.

great for __bronze__ skin!

#101

**Keep lips subtle
but shiny with
a bronzy**

NUDE
GLOSS.

#102
FIX FLYAWAYS

while you soothe your skin–after you've applied body lotion, run your fingers through your hair to smooth your strands.

#103

Mix one part concealer
with one part moisturizer
(in your hand) to create a

SHEER BASE—

it can take the place of a separate
lotion, concealer, and foundation.

#104

If your hair is curly, get

POUF-FREE ROOTS

by topping damp hair with a tight-fitting cap until dry.

great for curly hair

#105

To create a

HEALTHY GLOW,

dab cheeks with a sheer, rosy blush and smooth a cherry-colored gloss over lips.

great for golden skin!

#106

CREAMY PRODUCTS

give you the most natural look.
They blend easily into your skin
for a dewy, fresh complexion.

#107

Test a short style: Do a

TRIAL RUN

by pinning up the ends of
long hair to create a faux bob.

FRIZZ-EASE®

CARE

CURL AROUND™

Style-Starting
Daily Shampoo

Awakens & improves
natural curl patterns
for shiny, salon-style
spirals; hydrates,
nourishes & glosses.

CURLY

10 FL. OZ. (295 mL)

108

Bring out

WAVES

in straight hair—
use a curl enhancing
shampoo but skip
conditioner and
let it air-dry.

*great for
straight hair!*

#109

If you have

COARSE HAIR

on your legs, opt for waxing—
it will grow back thinner
and slower.

QUICK & EASY

WAX STRIPS

legs & body

ALL HAIR TYPES

EXPRESS →

16 (8 x 2 sided) strips

#110

Mix a few drops of **HONEY** with your regular shampoo, then wash and rinse hair well. It'll leave your strands extra soft and smooth.

great for oily skin

#111

EXFOLIATE

once a week, and more often if you have oily or flaky skin. Even though skin naturally sheds dead cells, it doesn't always do it fast enough to keep pores clear.

#112

Coloring your hair for the first time? If you have very long, thick hair, buy

TWO BOXES OF COLOR.

One box won't be enough to cover every strand.

#113

LOOK DEWY

without makeup—
after washing and
exfoliating your face,
apply moisturizer
while your skin is
still damp.

great for dry skin!

#114

LIP BALM

with dimethicone or glycerol will seal in moisture and keep your lips softer longer.

#115

If your skin is
combination
or oily, use

FACIAL MASKS

before you shower.
If it's dry, use them
afterward when
your skin is moist.

#116

Use elastics with

RUBBER GRIPS

to secure a ponytail to keep
your style from sliding out.

#117

"CORAL LIPSTICK can double as blush. Dab it on cheeks for a sunny glow."
– Matiki Anoff, makeup artist

#118

After cleansing your face,

OPEN PORES

by standing over a sink of steaming hot water for two minutes.

#119

BRAIDS
are a low-maintenance
way to get a new look.

#120

Turn off the shower while you use a

BODY SCRUB

so it doesn't get washed away before it has a chance to work.

#121

Go at least one day without washing your hair—the oils your scalp produces act as

NATURAL CONDITIONERS.

#122

BRONZE
makeup shades
make your skin
look radiant, not
washed out.

#123
SOOTHE
irritated skin with a cool, milk-soaked washcloth.

#124

An easy

OVERNIGHT CURE

for dry hands:
apply cream and
cover them with socks.

great for dry hair!

#125

For deeper conditioning,

APPLY AND COVER HAIR

with plastic wrap. Blast your head
with a blow-dryer for five minutes.
Leave the plastic wrap
on for another five, then rinse.

#126

Make thick hair feel lighter by having

CHOPPY LAYERS

cut into it.

#127

Mix

SELF-TANNER

with liquid foundation
to give your face a radiant,
natural-looking tan.

#128

GET BANGS—

at home: hold scissors
straight and upright, then
snip off at brow level.

great for <u>fair</u> skin!

#129

SHIMMERY,
muted makeup shades with peach undertones illuminate a paler complexion.

#130

To make cheeks glow use
SHEER LIPSTICK
in place of blush.

#131

Dab a little

LIP GLOSS

on your eyelids
just below the crease
to add shine for a
pretty, glossy look.

#132
Always schedule a
CONSULTATION
with your stylist before
committing to a
drastic haircut.

#133

If your skin tone is deep,

EARTH TONES,

like brick, add a bit of color
that won't look over powering.

great for
bronze/deep skin!

great for fine hair!

#134

If your hair is fine,
PERM
just your roots
to add body–
they'll look fuller,
not curly.

great for *fair skin!*

#135

A PINKISH GEL BLUSH

blends with your red undertones and gives you a pretty "I'm blushing" look.

#136
GET A TRIM
every 4 to 6 weeks
to keep curls bouncy.

#137

CLEAN

your shower pouf once a week to remove bacteria. Toss it into the washing machine with fragrance-free laundry detergent, then just let it air-dry.

#138
AVOID HAIR BREAKAGE—
coat your hair elastic with conditioner; *then* use it.

#139

To get the most

NATURAL-LOOKING

flush, apply cream blush to cheeks then put a tinted moisturizer *over* it. The blush will look like it's coming from within.

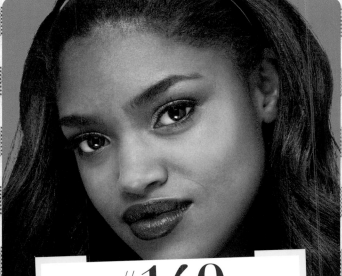

#140

Keep

PROCESSED HAIR

healthy by relaxing and coloring *just* the growth—not your whole head.

#141

Use masks instead of scrubs to avoid irritating your skin if it's

SENSITIVE.

great for <u>sensitive</u> skin!

#142

Apply liquid foundation with a fluffy

POWDER BRUSH

for natural coverage that's
not too cakey.

#143

FIGHT FLAKES—

let dandruff shampoo penetrate your scalp for at least five minutes before rinsing.

#144

Enhance the glossiness of your hair with

OLIVE OIL.

Smooth a tablespoonful on damp hair. Wait five minutes, and shampoo and condition as usual.

#145

To

ENHANCE

your hair color, use
a color-depositing
shampoo weekly.

#146

Best time to
color your hair red:

WINTER!

Red is the fastest
color to fade in
the summer sun.

#147

Put a sheer, honey-colored gloss on your lips to give them a natural-looking

SHEEN.

great for golden skin!

great for fair skin!

#148

Create a glistening, natural look with a shimmery
WHITE EYE SHADOW.

#149
HYDRATE

dry hair: mash two avocados in a bowl, then slather onto locks; leave on for 10 minutes and wash out completely.

#150

WASH
your hair brushes
each month with
soap and water
to clean off dirt
and oil buildup.

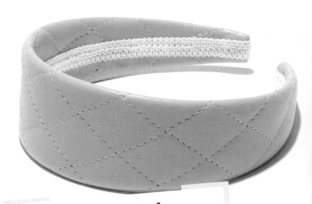

#151

Tuck short bangs under a

WIDE HEADBAND

if you're trying to grow them out.

#152

MICROWAVE

a small bowl of your body moisturizer for 20 seconds before you apply it—warm lotion is great for soothing tired muscles and dry feet.

FORMULA N°105
MOISTURIZING
BODY MILK
HONEY & SHEA

LE COUVENT DES MINIMES
HAUTE · PROVENCE

125 ML 4.2 FL.OZ

#153

To prevent
DYE STAINS
on your skin,
apply petroleum
jelly around your
hairline before
coloring your hair.

#154

Use a

CLAY MASK

once a month before your
period to help prevent acne.

great for
<u>*acne-prone*</u> *skin!*

party

A party or dance is the perfect time to try
a more daring look, like smoky eyes or a wild
hairstyle. You're going out and it's all about fun!
The beauty hints in this section will help
you make a red-carpet entrance every time!

17 TIP
Even when
you're going all out
remember to balance
new beauty tricks
with a few of your
old standbys.

#155

Use a tiny bit of sheer, silvery

HIGHLIGHTER

on your nose, cheeks, and browbones to define your features and make them stand out.

#156
USE A MOISTURIZER
containing light-reflecting particles
to add a subtle glow to your skin.

#157

PREVENT FRIZZ

by styling hair in an air-conditioned room. It'll help it look and feel sleek before you step outside.

#158

Wear

OIL-FREE FOUNDATION

if you have oily or combination skin. Less grease on your face means less shine, purer pores, and makeup that won't slide off.

great for oily skin →

Bespoke Labs

#159
If you have thicker hair
BLOWDRY
at a low- to medium-
setting. Hot air sucks moisture
from hair, making it flatter.

#160

To get the most

SATURATED COLOR,

use a flat shadow brush and *press* the shadow on eyes from lids to creases.

#161
SECOND DAY HAIR
is easier to style for updos—it will stay in place longer.

#162

"SMOKY EYES
are a big statement, so go natural
with the rest of your makeup."
– Gita Bass, makeup artist

#163

Try

BOLD EYELINER

colors, like electric blue or lime green, to make your eyes stand out against your skin.

great for golden/bronze and deep tones!

#164

Don't forget to add black mascara to finish off a

DRAMATIC

smoky eye look.

#165

To get that
professional-looking

SMUDGE,

apply cream or gel color
all around your eyes,
then squint once tightly.

#166

"**NEVER TOUCH** your face with your hands—the oils on them will melt your makeup! If you're dancing and sweating, gently blot your face with a paper napkin or tissue."
– Kristofer Buckle, celebrity makeup artist

#167

For the most intense
eye look, wear

BLACK LINER—
it's perfect for all skin tones.

great for prom!

#168

The morning of a big night out, comb deep conditioner through damp, clean hair and wrap your head with a towel. Leave in for 7 to 10 minutes. Then rinse with cool water for

ADDED SHINE.

#169
ALWAYS USE LIPLINER
to keep red lipstick in place.

#170

"CLIP-ON EXTENSIONS are the easiest way to get a glamorous hairstyle you might not be able to achieve with your own hair."
– Danilo, L.A.-based celebrity hairstylist

#171

Dab shimmery champagne or platinum gloss on the center of your lips over any lipstick color. It'll reflect light to

MAKE LIPS LOOK PLUMPER.

#172
Wrap a
SECOND ELASTIC
around your ponytail
for a style that won't
budge all night.

#173

When wearing dark
eye makeup, apply

METALLIC GOLD

shadow to the inner corners of
your eyes to open them up.

#174

To get your ends

STICK-STRAIGHT,

turn them outward with your
brush as you blow-dry.

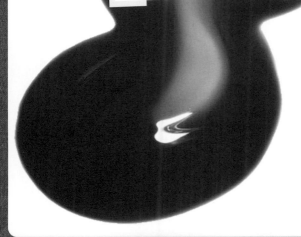

#175

To get

LONG-LASTING

red lips, apply cream concealer to
lips, then brush on lipstick.
Blot, and apply more color.

great for <u>*straight*</u> *hair!*

#176

For
LASTING CURLS
**(in straight hair),
use a small-barreled
iron. Tight curls
won't loosen as fast.**

#177

MAKE CRIMPED WAVES

without heat styling by sleeping in tight braids. Make two-to three-inch-wide braids in damp, clean hair.

#178

For the most

GLAM LIQUID-LINED EYES,

start the line out thin at your inner corners and gradually make it thicker as you paint it across your lids.

#179

Make freshly
washed hair

EASIER

to put up–give it grip
by applying mousse
while it's damp,
then let it air-dry
before styling.

#180

When creating a

DARK SMOKY EYE,

apply shadow with a sponge tip
applicator instead of a brush.
It will prevent the shadow from
crumbling onto your cheeks.

#181

Spray on your

FRAGRANCE

within seconds of
exiting the shower to
really absorb the scent.

#182

If your

DARK LIPSTICK

smudges as you apply it, dip a
cotton swab into a little concealer or
face powder to cover the stain.

#183

AVOID DAMAGE—

spritz your almost-air-dried
hair with heat-protective spray
before blow-drying to finish.

#184

Even if you have oily skin you should

MOISTURIZE—

it will improve the texture of your skin and reduce the appearance of pores.

great for oily skin

#185

APPLY A TOP COAT

every other day to make your manicure last.

#186
GIVE ROOTS A LIFT
by pulling a round brush up through your hair toward the ceiling as you blow-dry.

#187

Avoid ending up with

CLUMPS OF PRODUCT

in your hair by applying it to bottom layers first, *then* to top layers.

#188

Remove any items from your bag that you'll need after you get a professional manicure, like money and car keys—that way you won't

SMUDGE YOUR NAILS.

great for prom!

#189

PREVENT PIMPLES

by washing your makeup brushes with a gentle shampoo once a month to get rid of bacteria and oil buildup.

#190

"Red lipstick makes you

LOOK CONFIDENT

and ready for anything."
– Poppy King, makeup artist and
Color Designer for Prescriptives

#191

Always apply your makeup by **NATURAL** (OR GOOD) **LIGHT** so you see exactly how much you're putting on.

#192

HELP BLEMISHES

or skin discoloration on your body look less noticeable with a gold-flecked lotion. Use on bare skin, then wait 10 minutes before you dress.

#193

"START EVERY UP-DO with a ponytail—it provides a strong base for any style."
– Ken Paves, celebrity hair stylist

#194

GIVE YOUR LASHES

a "false lash" look by
curling them gently *after*
applying mascara.

#195

To get a

HEALTHY GLOW,

mix a dime-size dollop of tinted self-tanner with the same amount of moisturizer and apply to your face a few days before prom.

great for prom! →

Neutrogena

sun fresh™

sunless foam

FAIR/MEDIUM SKIN TONES

GRAPEFRUIT · NECTARINE

sheer summer color with a delicious, fresh scent

4.0 FL OZ (118 mL)

#196

"CHUNKY
HIGHLIGHTS
are a fun way to play with
your natural color."
– Kris Sorbie, colorist

#197

If your dress exposes
your back, have Mom

CAMOUFLAGE

any body breakouts with
concealer the same way
you would on your face.

great for prom!

#198

For great results,

FLATIRON

sections of hair that are the same width as the iron.

great for prom!

#199

Wait until your deodorant dries completely before getting dressed. Even **"INVISIBLE" FORMULAS** can leave white marks on your dress. If this happens, brush it off with a dry washcloth.

#200

Combat a shiny face by using

MATTIFYING GEL

on forehead, nose, and chin.

great for prom!

#201

PICK A NAIL SHADE

one notch lighter *or* darker than your dress to complement the color."

– Elle, celebrity manicurist

#202

To prevent damage,
don't leave a hot tool on
your hair for more than

10 SECONDS.

great for oily skin →

#203

The best way to

TEASE HAIR

without damaging it is to comb it gently in *one* direction—toward your roots, not back and forth.

#204

If you're not sure which

LONG-LASTING

lipstick color to wear, test them before prom night—they shouldn't wipe off easily.

great for prom!

#205

For styles that

WON'T BUDGE,

use thickening spray (a volume-boosting product) it offers the best staying power.

JOHN FRIEDA
london · paris · new york

sheer
blonde.

Full-Blown Blonde®
volumizing spray

THICKENS
LIFTS

brightens blonde
instantly thickens &
lifts fine, thin, delicate
blonde for full, lush
results

body-enhancing formula
plumps up strands;
locks in lasting lift
boosts shine

for natural, color-treated
or highlighted blondes

6.7 FL. OZ. (200 mL)

#206

Keep

TWO SHADES

of foundation on hand—
one for winter when you're
paler and one for summer
when you're bronzed.

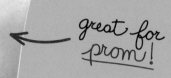

great for prom!

the
SANCTUARY
SPA COVENT GARDEN

Relax & indulge your body
with Natural Pumice
Orange & [...]
to invigora[...]
moistur[...]

Body Scru[...]

200ml ℮ 6.7 fl[...]

#207

EXFOLIATE

your body every other day
in the month leading up to
prom for a bumpless back.
Use a gentle body scrub
that sloughs off dry skin
and clears oil-clogged pores.

#208

Once your self-tanner has dried
(about five minutes), perfect it
with a light application of

SHIMMER LOTION

or oil. This will help
camouflage any goof-ups.

great for prom!

#209

Instead of using lipliner to define your pout
(it can look harsh),

USE TWO LIPSTICKS

in slightly different shades. Apply the
darker shade on the outer edges of your lips
and the lighter one to fill in the middle.

#210

Dress up short styles with a fun, jewel-encrusted

HEADBAND.

great for thick hair!

#211

"Two weeks before prom, **SPOT-TEST** self-tanner on the back of your arm to make sure it doesn't streak or turn your skin orange."
– Mally Roncal, celebrity makeup artist

#212

To apply mascara to your bottom lashes, tilt your head forward and look up. You'll have

MORE CONTROL.

#213

To make lipstick stick longer to your lips,

BLOT

with a piece of tissue before applying another coat.

#214

Don't forget to keep an

INSTANT
OIL-ABSORBING
sheet in your purse on prom night.

great for prom!

#215

"Evening looks don't need to be complex—red lips or subtle shimmer add

INSTANT INTENSITY."

- Jo Strettell, celebrity makeup artist.

#216

To avoid

HELMET HEAD,

spritz hairspray on your palms, then pat your hair.

#217

Use

CREAM

foundation as a base for eyeshadow to help it stay put.

#218

Use jeweled

FALSE LASHES

for a fun night out—it will give
a little twinkle to your eyes.

great for fair skin!

heer Lipgloss
Brillant à lèvres
translucide
0.34 fl oz
10ml

#219

A candy-colored pink pout with bright blue liner is fun, flirty, and

EYE-CATCHING.

#220

When you decide what to do withyour hair

FOR PROM

consider going half—it's elegant
but still feels fun.

#221
To avoid
NAIL-ART OVERKILL,
try a design or crystal on only one nail, like on your index or middle finger.

great for prom!

#222

APPLY PINK GLOSS

to the middle of your top and bottom lip, then rub together—this will make gloss go on evenly without getting goopy.

#223

Pump up the
VOLUME
for a special occasion
with a deep side
part and curls!

great for
deep-set eyes!

#224

Make deep-set eyes

STAND OUT

with a shimmery, silver/gray shadow.

#225

DARK NAVY EYELINER

is striking with soft
pink lips and cheeks.

#226

Keep eye makeup

SUBTLE

when you wear false lashes.

#227

USE MINI BOBBY PINS

**when doing an updo—
they're easier to hide,
so your style, not
your pins, standout.**

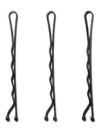

#228

To get more intensity out of your
eyeshadow, use a damp cotton swab to apply

SHADOW AS LINER.

#229

Pair smoky eyes with

PINK CHEEKS

and lips for a
rocker-meets-debutante look.

great for prom!

#230

Brighten your natural hair color or color-treated hair by alternating your regular shampoo with one that's

COLOR-ENHANCING

for a few weeks before prom.

#231

BEFORE

buying eyeliner, draw a few lines with the sample on your hand so that you know how it will go onto your lids.

TAN
AIRBRUSH
IN A CAN

TRANSLUCENT
FORMULA

SELF-TANNING SPRAY
FOR FACE AND BODY
WITH 360° NOZZLE

Spray auto-bronzant
instantané pour visage
et corps-buse à 360°

150g / 210ml net ℮

MODEL co

#232

Use an aerosol

SPRAY BRONZER—

once the formula dries, it won't smudge the *entire* night. Spray it onto the back of your hand, then use a foundation brush to sweep it onto cheeks.

#233

For pretty,
SHIMMERY SKIN ALL-OVER,
mix one teaspoon each of
baby oil and shimmer powder
with 1/2 cup body lotion,
then apply apply on your body
or on exposed areas.

#234

Dab on an orange-based red lipstick, starting in the center of your lips. It looks festive *and* makes

TEETH LOOK WHITER.

great for prom!

#235

Make foundation

LAST
EXTRA
LONG

**by patting loose
powder on top.**

#236

To give your daytime look

NIGHTTIME DRAMA,

line your top lids with liquid liner
(wing out the corners), then slick
on shiny clear lip gloss.

#237

For a

VIBRANT KISSER,

dab your gloss on the center of
your mouth, then work it outward
with a lip brush for precision.

great for prom!

#238

Slide a

TINY TIARA

in at the top of a French-rolled
bun to dress up your look.

#239

Shimmery shadow is a perfect—and easy!—

PARTY LOOK.

#240
ALWAYS REMOVE
eye makeup at night—leaving it on can cause irritation and even infection.

#241

"Before a special occasion, wash your hair with bottled water— its pH balance will

BOOST THE SHINE!"

– Robert Lyon, celebrity hairstylist

#242

Nails with a metallic
finish will give you an

EDGY LOOK

without seeming overdone.

#243

If you're doing

DARK EYE MAKEUP,

do that before you apply any other makeup (even foundation), then finish your face. It will help you judge how much blush and lipgloss you need.

#244

A loose,

TOUSLED BUN

is easy and fun
for a night out.

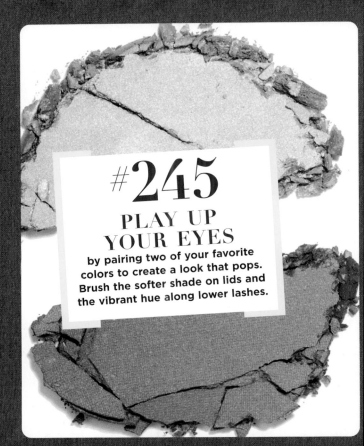

#245

PLAY UP YOUR EYES

by pairing two of your favorite colors to create a look that pops. Brush the softer shade on lids and the vibrant hue along lower lashes.

#246

Make sure your style is

REALLY SECURE

before you leave the house. After styling your hair, shake your head from side to side–then fix any pieces that fall or feel loose.

#247

Smudge eyeliner with a shadow brush to get a sexy,

SMOKY EFFECT.

#248

Use

JET-BLACK

liquid liner to draw a line over the base of the false lashes—it will camouflage them *and* add more drama.

#249

"BE CAREFUL

when you hug or kiss someone hello. I tell my
clients to make sure they don't let their hair touch
the person they're hugging—it'll mess up
their style."– Ken Paves, celebrity hair stylist

#250

Sweep

POWDER EYESHADOW

(in a similar color) over your eyeliner to keep it from smudging.

#251

Deep, dark nail colors like purple, red, and black—painted just on your tips—create a sexy new take on the

FRENCH MANICURE.

#252

Wear a

SIDE PONY

secured with multiple elastics
down the tail for a cool, rocker
update on a basic style.

#253

TWO-TONED

metallic eyeshadow—silver on the top, gold along the bottom—looks decadent and utterly glamorous.

#254

PHOTO LIGHTS

exaggerate shine. Use a little matte-finish foundation to get an even, shine-free complexion.

great for prom!

#255

One reason to use vibrant shadow, liner, or mascara: It gives your eyes a glamorous,

JEWEL-LIKE EFFECT

that sparkles.

#256

MATCH

your lip color to your shoes (especially if they are a different color than your dress) for celeb-worthy look.

great for prom!

#257

Spray firm-hold aerosol hairspray onto a toothbrush, using it to clean up

STRAY HAIRS

along your hairline and part.

Herbal essences

PIN STRAIGHT MOUSSE

WITH A FUSION OF

honeyed pear
&
silk

I love it when you get straight to the point

NET WT. 6.8 OZ (192 g

#258

Breathe new life into a simple pony—tie it high on your crown and tease the top for some

PLAYFUL HEIGHT.

date

Whether you're going on an official dinner date or just hanging out, the hair and makeup tricks in this chapter will help you show off your flirty, girly side.

17 TIP

Avoid wearing intense colors (especially on lips!) and too much hair product on dates—most guys prefer the natural look.

#259

If you are trying a
daring new look, do a

PRACTICE
RUN

the night before to
make sure you are
comfortable with it.

#260

Before applying makeup, put on a lightweight

PRIMER

to keep it in place. Bonus: It smoothes the texture of your skin.

#261

To make

HIGHLIGHTS LOOK BRIGHT,

rub a dime-sized amount of pomade in your hands and apply it to the ends of your hair.

#262
A CORAL BLUSH
applied to the apples brightens a dull complexion.

#263

For

SEXY LASHES

swipe one coat of lengthening mascara on your top and bottom lashes. Let that dry, then apply a coat of thickening mascara over it.

#264

Give your complexion a

HEALTHY ROSINESS

by brushing blush onto the apples of your cheeks, then dusting your forehead, nose, and chin with the remaining color on the brush.

#265

GET SOFT LOCKS

by using the right amount of conditioner. Tight curls need 1 tablespoon (they're drier); loose curls need 2 teaspoons.

great for curly hair

#266
DON'T GO OVERBOARD!
Put bronzer only on areas the sun would normally hit: your cheeks, nose, and forehead.

#267
MAKE YOUR OWN
aromatherapy shampoo. Add 2 drops of an essential oil to a dollop of shampoo, then wash.

#268

If you style with a blow-dryer
and your brush bristles look
like they've melted, it's

TIME FOR A
NEW BRUSH.

#269

To create an extra-sexy

NIGHTTIME LOOK,

begin winging your liquid liner upward as you near the outer corners of your eye, but don't extend it past your outer corners.

#270
To keep lips looking

KISSABLE,
avoid wearing super sticky
lip gloss (it can look
goopy at times).

#271

Apply leave-in conditioner to your ends before styling to

MAKE HAIR EXTRA SOFT.

#272

A pretty

JEWELED HAIR CLIP

adds a flirty touch—
just stick to a single
color family if you're
wearing more than one.

great for
fine hair!

#273

**Flip your head over
as you blow-dry your
hair to add even more**

VOLUME AT
YOUR ROOTS.

#274

To make your eyes sparkle (especially in dim light), dab a shimmery

CHAMPAGNE SHADOW

on the inner and outer corners of your eyes and across browbones.

#275

DEFINED TEXTURE

is the key to making short hair sexy—use pomade or wax to bring out your layers.

great for <u>short</u> hair!

#276

Give your powder shadow a

CREAMY CONSISTENCY—

apply your shadow, then dip a Q-Tip
in lip balm and sweep it on top.

#277

EYES LOOK BIGGER

if you curl your lashes and add two coats of mascara after applying shadow, the excess shadow that falls on lashes gives them volume.

#278

To make fine hair look fluffy,

CONDITION FIRST,

then shampoo.

great for fine hair!

#279

To make a

LIPSTICK LAST,

apply one coat of lipstick, blot, then add another coat. Kiss a tissue to blot again, then lightly dust your mouth with translucent powder.

#280

Get soft,

FULL HAIR

**by using a light mousse
or gel that absorbs
slightly in your hands; it
prevents crunchy hair.**

great for <u>*brown eyes!*</u>

#281

NEUTRAL COLORS

like beige, cocoa brown, and
plummy brown pick up the flecks
of bronze in your eyes.

#282

Add a

SMIDGEN OF SHIMMER

to the center of each eyelid—it
will catch the light when you
blink to make your lids glimmer.

#283

Apply a matte

LIPSTICK

formula for the longest wear, creamy texture for hydration, and sheer for subtle color and shine.

great for
~~fine~~ hair!

#284

Make fine hair thicker by getting
highlights or all-over color—both

ADD TEXTURE
TO THIN LOCKS.

#285

For long-lasting, kissable lips, wear

GLOSS WITH GLITTER

in it. The flecks of shimmer stay on your lips even after the color fades.

#286

GET PRETTY CURLS—

make four braided ponytails around your head while hair is damp, and twist them into loose knots. When dry, let down the knots and unravel the braids.

#287

APPLY LIP PLUMPERS

before you put on any other makeup—so it has time to work. By the time you put on your lip color, the product will have taken effect.

#288

AVOID FLAT HAIR
by holding straightening irons at
least an inch away from your roots.

#289

For a

WIDE-EYED
FLIRTY LOOK,

always apply mascara to
both top and bottom lashes.

FLIRT! BIG FLIRT™
THICKENING
MASCARA

#290
SPEND MORE TIME
perfecting your skin with foundation than on applying other makeup—when your skin is even you won't need much other makeup.

#291

HELP ENDS FEEL SOFT

by not scrubbing when you shampoo, which dries them out.

#292

Use a

DRY TOOTHBRUSH

to gently scrub flaky bits of skin off
your lips before you apply lipstick.

#293

Make blonde hair

SHINY—

rinse with equal
parts lemon juice
and water once
a week to strip
residue.

#294

Purple eyeliner

ENHANCES

the whites of your eyes, making you look more awake. Fair skin tones should stick to lavender shades and darker skin tones to deep plums.

#295

Apply clear gloss over a lip stain for a

PRETTY FINISH.

#296

Wear liquid
foundation that has

LIGHT REFLECTIVE PARTICLES

in it for glowing,
candle-lit-looking skin.

#297

After cleansing, splash your face 10 times with cool water to get blood flowing and

MAKE SKIN GLOW.

great for
<u>green</u> eyes!

#298

Shades of purple contrast and

BRIGHTEN
GREEN EYES.

great for fair skin!

#299

HIDE DARK ROOTS

with dry white shampoo or even baby powder.

Johnson's®
baby powder

Keeps skin silky soft,
fresh & comfortable

Johnson&Johnson

NET WT 9 OZ (255g)

724360

#300

Make your own

SCENTED BODY LOTION—

put a dollop of the unscented kind in your hand, then spritz it with your favorite fragrance.

#301

Dust your collarbones, legs, and arms with shimmer powder if they are showing to

REALLY HIGHLIGHT THEM.

#302

ADD HIGHLIGHTS
around your face that are two
shades lighter than your
hair to brighten your complexion.

#303

SMUDGE

a bit of your eyeliner on the inner corners of your eyes for a sultry finish.

EYELINER · CRAYON TRACEUR
130 JEAN JACKET/VESTE DE DENIM

FACTOR

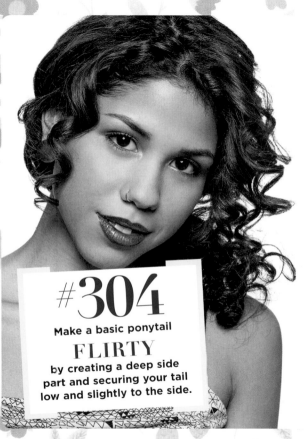

#304

Make a basic ponytail

FLIRTY

by creating a deep side part and securing your tail low and slightly to the side.

#305

To create

SOFT CURLS

blow-dry three-inch-wide sections with a round brush, always rolling it in toward your face.

#306
ADD SEXY MOTION
to your ends by having
your stylist give
them textured layers.

great for hazel eyes!

#307

Shades like

BRONZY GOLDS

and shimmery ambers highlight specks of gold, green, and brown in your eyes.

#308
Draw attention to
your eyes with

BANGS
cut below your brows.

#309

To

MAKE YOUR SCENT LAST,

use the bath and body products with the same fragrance.

#310

USE A LOOFAH
to apply body cleanser for
extra smoothing benefits.

#311

Deep red nails create a dazzling,

SOPHISTICATED LOOK.

#312

FLIRTY CURLS
shouldn't look perfect,
so place different sized rollers
randomly throughout hair.

great for dry skin!

#313

Put on a body lotion with

SHEA BUTTER

every morning. It's high in fatty acids—so it moisturizes skin well.

#314

Dab a little extra lip gloss on your cheeks and beneath your brows for a

SUBTLE GLOW.

#315

Make soft

DEFINED CURLS

by twisting and pinning small sections of hair to scalp. Leave in overnight.

#316

For a softer look, use your

SHADOW AS LINER:

put a drop of water on your slanted liner brush before swirling it in the shadow. Line as usual.

#317

Body scrub can double as a

FOOT BUFFER,

especially on rough heels.

#318

"IT'S OKAY TO MATCH

your eyeshadow to your top if the color is light but if it's crazy bright, like blue, it can be too much."
– Linday Hay, Victoria's Secret makeup artist

#319

Apply body lotion
within three minutes of
your bath or shower to

SEAL IN
MOISTURE.

#320
PAIR ROSY LIPS
and cheeks with smoky lids
for a glamorous look that's
easy to pull off.

kimble hair care systems™

BOUNCE BACK
CURLING REVITALIZER

Net Wt. 8 oz / 226 g

#321
ALWAYS START
with a little amount of hair product, you can always apply more!

#322

Warm, bronzy hues on your
eyes and cheeks and some
golden lip gloss gives you a

ROMANTIC GLOW.

great for golden skin!

great for blue eyes!

#323

An iridescent,
SILVER
eyeshadow brings out
light-colored eyes.

#324
FALSE EYELASHES
are an easy way to look glam.

great for curly hair

#325
Short ear- and chin-length layers can

ADD VOLUME
to wispy, fine hair.

#326

SLICK
jewel-toned polish
on toenails for a
fun effect.

#327

"Waves are carefree and
GLAMOROUS
at the same time."
– Nathaniel Hawkins,
celebrity hair stylist

342

#328

TEASE
YOUR HAIR
at the crown of your head for volume before sliding on a thin headband for a flirty finish.

great for fair skin!

#329

Dust a shimmery

PRESSED POWDER

onto your cheekbones
to highlight
them subtly.

#330

Give your everyday ponytail

SOME ATTITUDE

by using a chic jeweled chip.

#331

LOOSEN CURLS

by wrapping three-inch-wide sections of dry hair around large Velcro rollers. Use hairspray, wait 15 minutes— and remove.

great for curly hair

#332

TO ADD DRAMA

to your lashes and make them more striking, apply a coat of mascara to your top and bottom lashes and let dry. Apply a second coat to your top lashes only.

#333

SPICE UP YOUR LOOK

and create a tropical beauty effect by pinning a flower behind your ear or on your ponytail.

#334

Create

SMOLDERING EYES

using warm bronzy shadow (not
black or charcoal—they're too harsh).

#335

Keep cheeks and lips
natural-looking with

SOFT
PINKS.

#336

When you want a girly,

TOUSLED HAIRSTYLE—

not stiff hair that doesn't move—spritz hair with holding spray, then curl and style.

great for bronze skin!

#337

COPPER COLORS

work nicely with bronze skin for a look that's shimmery and sexy but still natural.

#338

WEAR FLAVORED LIP GLOSS—

when he gets close enough
he'll smell the sweet scent.

#339

Swipe your fingertip over a cream lipstick and then press it onto the center of your lips, blending outward—it'll give your lips a

FLIRTY STAIN.

#340

Piecey,
SIDESWEPT BANGS
give one length
hair a flirty vibe.

#341

For an update of old

HOLLYWOOD GLAMOUR,

create large curls all over with a curling iron, but then brush them out to soften the look.

#342

"KEEP YOUR MAKEUP SIMPLE

and you'll have more success with guys. They want to see who you are, so don't transform yourself too much."
– Linda Hay, Victoria's Secret makeup artist

#343

Apply mousse by squirting it onto a vent brush and then gliding it through your hair. It will give you pretty

VOLUME ALL OVER.

358

#344

To turn your natural makeup into a

FLIRTY DATE LOOK,

add silvery-blue shadow from your lids
to creases, then swipe on black mascara.

perle

*great for
fair skin!*

great for
<u>round face</u>
shapes

#345

When wearing a pretty, voluminous style, pull your hair back into an updo—the sleek sides will

ELONGATE YOUR FACE.

#346

ACCENTUATE

**the shape of your eyes
with a graphic swipe
of electric blue liner—
it's edgy, not trampy.**

#347

Curling your hair with the barrel slightly closed

PREVENTS CREASES

from forming.

great for <u>blue</u> eyes!

#348

PEARLY PINKS,
peaches, and corals contrast with
blue eyes to make their color pop.

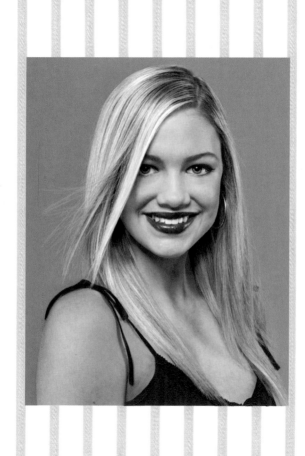

work

Let your boss know you take your work seriously by keeping your look polished — the suggestions in this section will help you master sophisticated makeup and glossy, healthy hair.

17 TIP
Keep makeup colors on the neutral side and leave complicated hairstyles for after school jobs.

#349

Get smooth waves if you
have curly hair by

BLOWDRYING

on cool to seal the
cuticle and set the curl.

great for curly hair

#350

APPLY YOUR BRONZER

with a soft, fluffy brush to get the most natural-looking color on your skin.

essence of BEAUTY®

#351

REVIVE LIMP HAIR

with dry shampoo between washings to add texture and mask grease.

#352

Use a lengthening mascara formula, it goes on thinner than other formulas so it

ADDS DEFINITION

to your eyes without looking clumpy.

#353

Get a

HAIR STYLE

that suits *you*—bring celebrity photos you like to your stylist. If your face shape is different, she can adjust the cut.

#354

Use only

METAL-FREE HAIR ELASTICS.

Hair bands fastened together with metal clasps tend to rip hair when you remove them.

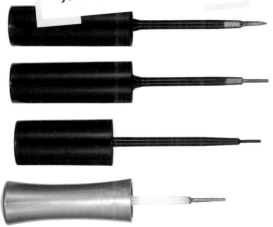

#355

Get

DEFINED EYES

that still look utterly natural by
applying liquid liner as close to
your top lash line as possible.

372

#356

Keep long, thin hair full of healthy-looking body with a cut that's

LAYERED ALL OVER.

#357

SPOT APPLY

moisturizer only where you're dry. Oil is a natural hydrator, so oily skin doesn't need a dose of moisturizer—just on dry patches.

great for combo skin

#358

Keep your brows

LOOKING POLISHED

by brushing them upward, then holding them in place with brow gel.

#359

To make hair look
healthier when it
needs to be cut,

CURL YOUR
ENDS UNDER

with a round brush
while blow-drying.

#360

Some say caffeine

MAKES HAIR LIMP —
so try to limit how much you drink!

#361

Wear shimmery products on only
two features (like eyes and lips)
to keep your makeup clean and

PROFESSIONAL.

#362

For redheads, auburn-colored

BROW FILLERS

look unnatural. Use a blonde pencil instead.

#363

BE GENTLE

when washing acne-prone skin. Aggressive scrubbing can inflame pimples even more.

great for acne-prone skin!

A fluid gel cleanser for all skin types. Formulated with vegetable soap substitutes, the White tea fluid gel deeply cleanses and refreshes, without dehydrating the skin. The gel is very concentrated; yet the Oat proteins form a moisturising film protecting the skin. The selected vegetable extracts contain flavonoids...

LOT. 0509013
EXP. 03/2008

#364

Apply

PRESSED POWDER

to shiny areas of your skin only, not all over, so your skin looks fresh but not pancake-like.

#365

BROWN HAIR DYES

(more than others) can come out looking dull if hair isn't healthy. So deep condition once a week for a month, and get a trim before you color.

#366

Apply bright eyeliner *softly* to your bottom lashes so that it looks like thick lashes, not a line of

OBVIOUS MAKEUP.

#367

For a
**PERFECT
CENTER
LINE,**
part your hair
with a comb,
then blow-dry.

#368

For pretty,

TOTALLY
NATURAL COLOR,
use a neutral pencil to line your
lips *and* fill them in. Then just
apply clear gloss on top.

#369
FIGHT FRIZZY CURLS:
Use humectant-free gel, which fights moisture, on roots—the first area to frizz.

#370

Keep eye gel/cream in the fridge—
the cold helps further

REDUCE PUFFINESS
by constricting the blood vessels.

#371

Eat at least

FIVE OUNCES OF PROTEIN

a day to give hair lots of shine!

great for fine hair!

#372

Keep fine hair

FULL OF BODY

by using leave-in conditioner instead of heavier in-the-shower types.

#373

You should have

TWO CONCEALERS,

one that matches your skin exactly to cover pimples and a second that is a shade lighter for under your eyes.

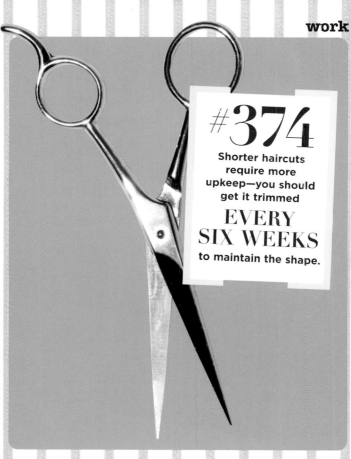

#374

Shorter haircuts require more upkeep—you should get it trimmed

EVERY SIX WEEKS

to maintain the shape.

#375

To make red lipstick

SHEERER,

apply a thin coat of lip balm, then press red lipstick into your lips using your finger.

#376

AFTER SHAMPOOING

be sure to rinse your hair very well (for about two minutes). Any cleansing product left in your hair can make it look dull.

#377

SWEEP BRONZER
with a soft, fluffy brush to get the most
natural-looking color on your skin.

#378
HOLD YOUR BLOW-DRYER
six inches away, so you don't burn and damage your hair.

#379

After lining the inner rims of your eyes with liner, line a bit of powder shadow along your lash line to

KEEP THE PENCIL FROM SMUDGING.

great for curly hair

#380

If you have thick or curly hair, don't rinse conditioner out completely–leaving a tiny bit behind will keep your hair

SOFT ALL DAY.

#381

Try a

FRAGRANCE ALTERNATIVE —

spray perfume onto your hair. Hair actually holds onto fragrance longer.

FLIRTATIOUS!

#382

"LOWLIGHTS
add pretty, subtle
depth to your hair."
– Chuck Hezekiah, Garnier
hair color expert

#383

When
APPLYING SHADOW,
start at the outer corners of your eyes and work in. Keep the outer corners darkest and inner corners lightest.

#384

LOCK IN SHINE
by mixing 2 tablespoons white vinegar with 1 cup warm water. Pour over clean, wet hair, then rinse with cool water.

#385

Before applying blush
think about where you

NATURALLY FLUSH

and swipe the
blush on those areas.

#386

Comb through your lashes after applying mascara to make sure they are

CLUMP FREE.

great for straight hair!

#387

For MAXIMUM SHINE, use a boar-bristle brush on straight hair; it helps distribute natural oils throughout.

#388

SPRITZ HAIRSPRAY

onto your brush before
brushing for a soft hold.

#389

For ends that

REMAIN CURLED,

blow-dry with a round brush, and hold hair around the brush until cool.

DERMABLEND

D

Smoo...
Indulg...

CONCEA...

ONG LAS...
MATTE FINISH...

0.3 fl oz (... ...L)

#390

Apply your makeup in

MULTIPLE THIN LAYERS:

it's the secret to
getting it right

#391

Avoid

OBVIOUS

roots—put highlights below top
layers (instead of on top) so
color peeks through.

#392

Pop your gel eyeliner in the fridge before using it to get a more PRECISE LINE.

#393

Brighten brown hair—brew two cups of sage tea, let tea cool, pour onto clean hair, and rinse. Sage's rich hue will

WARM UP YOUR COLOR.

great for brown hair

410

#394

IF YOU'VE HAD A LONG DAY,
dust on a touch of bronzy pink blush to perk you up.

#395

Get

STRAIGHTER HAIR

by aiming the nozzle of your blow-dryer in the same direction you're pulling hair.

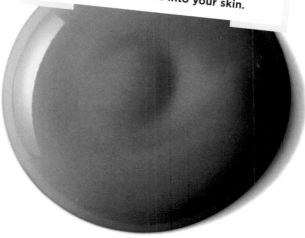

#396

Your perfect

FOUNDATION SHADE

should disappear into your skin. Test three shades on your jawline—go with the one that melts into your skin.

great for blonde hair!

#397

For natural-looking blonde or

BRUNETTE BROWS,

use a powder or a pencil that is two shades lighter than your own color.

#398

Style your hair at
night, then sleep with
a silk scarf wrapped
around your head to

MAKE THE
LOOK LAST.

great for
fair skin!

#399

A sheer,

BERRY GLOSS

gives a pale complexion just enough color without overpowering it.

NEW
Clean & Clear®
OIL-FR
Oxygen
ULTRA-L
MOISTUR
Moisturizes and
For visibly health
SPF 15
Johnson
4 FL. OZ.
7248

#400
NEED A FRIZZ-FIGHTER?
If you run out of hair stuff, lightly glaze the top layer of your hair with a dime-size amount of lotion.

#401
PLUM BLUSH SHADES
look more sophisticated (and mature) than pinks.

#402

When you don't have
TIME TO PLUCK,
cover up baby hairs beneath
your brows with concealer.

#403

If your hair is

RELAXED,

sleep on a satin or silk pillowcase to keep it shiny—cotton absorbs moisture and oil from your hair, making it dry.

#404

Use a

THIN HEADBAND

to hold back short layers of hair.

#405

Apply

BROWN LINER

to lash lines to make light lashes look darker and thicker.

great for dark hair!

422

great for bronze skin!

#406
Tan skin looks fresh and just-pinched
(not doll-like and overdone) in
BRIGHT PINK BLUSH.

great for golden skin!

#407

**For a little pop, define
your eyes, with a**

DEEP PLUM LINER

instead of black or brown.

#408

A pinkish-red

STAIN

applied to your lips and the apples of your cheeks gives you a natural-but-polished look that's sophisticated *and* professional.

#409

An eyeshadow
brush with a

SPONGEY TIP

blends shadow
more softly and
smoothly than one
with a straight tip.

#410

SHOW OFF YOUR FACE

with this chic style: part hair on the side and tuck it behind your ears. Keep it smooth with a gel.

#411

A metallic,

SHIMMERY MANICURE,

looks chic and sophisticated.

#412

If you get bumps above or below your brows after plucking, apply an acne spot treatment with

SALICYLIC ACID

to zap them.

#413

"For the most natural look, dot eyeliner pencil between each of your top lashes to

SUBTLY DEFINE

your eyes."
– Bobbi Brown, makeup artist

414

For a polished
everyday look,
use a large-barreled
curling iron to

FLIP OUT
YOUR ENDS.

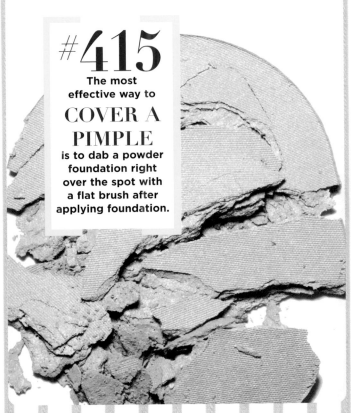

#415

The most effective way to

COVER A PIMPLE

is to dab a powder foundation right over the spot with a flat brush after applying foundation.

#416
A BLUNT BOB
that falls below your jawline is
sophisticated and super-flattering
for oval face shapes.

#417

When crunched for time, slick on a bold

COLORED LIPSTICK

and nothing else, for an
instant pulled-together look.

#418

Rub a dime-sized amount of hair wax between your palms, then run your hands down your ponytail to

SMOOTH FLYAWAYS.

#419

Use a

POWDER FOUNDATION

for a flawless-looking complexion. Semi-matte skin is professional and clean looking.

great for oily skin

#420

MAKE HAIR LOOK CHIC

and glossy by slicking it into a low, sleek bun with hair gel (light reflects off it).

#421

If you don't have time to do a full manicure,

SWIPE ON A CLEAR COAT

to keep your nails looking great.

ADHERES
NAIL
COLOR

BASECOAT anchor

ZOYA

.5 oz /15ml

#422

Apply cream blush with a

BLUSH BRUSH

for a more evenly distributed, soft finish.

#423

If you have a more

FINISHED HAIRSTYLE,

keep your makeup
very natural
to avoid looking
too overdone.

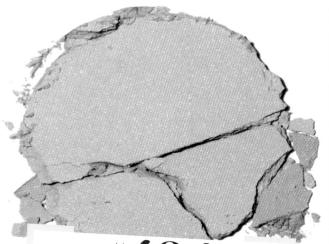

#424

Don't dust on

TOO MUCH POWDER

throughout the day or else your makeup
will look cakey instead of polished.

#425

Stash hand lotion in your bag to

KEEP HANDS HYDRATED

in air-conditioned places.

#426

When wearing your hair in a ponytail,
secure it with an elastic that

MATCHES YOUR HAIR COLOR.

#427

SKIP OPEN-TOED SHOES

if your feet look like they are in need of a pedicure.

#428

In a pinch, instantly make ragged split ends look better by rubbing a *tiny*

DAB OF OLIVE OIL

on them.

#429

Apply a zit treatment directly on pimple in the

A.M. AND P.M. —

any more and you'll risk drying out your skin.

OLE HENRIKSEN

Roll–On Blemish Attack
Solution aux Imperfections
En applicateur à bille

.35 Fl. Oz./10.3ml e

#430
Keep your bangs out of your face while you work with **BOBBY PINS** that match your hair color.

#431

Wear

DARK
BLUE
MASCARA

**to make your
eyes look brighter.**

great for
bronze/deep/skin!

#432

PLUM COLORS

all over add a gorgeous warmth to deep skin tones to make your features stand out.

#433

Wear cream or

LIQUID FOUNDATION,

they are more moisturizing so your skin won't look dried out and look more natural.

great for dry skin!

#434

Stash a

MISTING SPRAY

in your bag and spritz your face a couple of times during the day to keep skin and makeup looking fresh.

#435

**Apply bright shadows as close
to lash lines as possible to**

PREVENT CREASING.

#436

Use a medium-sized foundation brush to apply base for a sheer, but

POLISHED FINISH.

Blend it with an X motion to prevent brush marks.

pool

When you hit the pool or beach, you have to protect your skin from the sun and your hair from chlorine. That doesn't mean you can't have fun with things like shimmer and bronzer; however — they help you look glam all summer long.

17 TIP
Stick to sheer makeup and fuss-free hair that looks laid-back, but pretty.

#439

FIX POST-BEACH HAIR

by cleansing it with conditioner instead of shampoo. Then wash your hair as usual the following morning.

#440

Wear sunscreen with
self-tanner in it to

ACCENTUATE
YOUR TAN

and give your body
a slimmer look.

#441
REMOVE BUILD-UP
from salt and chlorine: Rinse wet hair once a week with 1/4 cup apple-cider vinegar mixed with a cup of water before shampooing.

#442

If your

WATERPROOF MASCARA

seems runny, apply one coat
of regular mascara first then
add a layer of waterproof
for perfectly defined lashes.

#443

PREVENT BREAKAGE
by blotting (not rubbing) hair dry with a towel.

#444

LESS MAKEUP IS MORE

at the beach. You'll need to reapply sunscreen and reapplying over makeup feels gunky and can clog pores.

#445

For a quick

SLEEK UPDO
(and damage control!)
use a dollop of
sunscreen to style.

#446

"Spritz skin with seawater—the salt makes it

LOOK DEWY

after the water dries."
– Ann Marie, makeup artist

#447

If you're going outside,
bandage any hair-removal-induced

NICKS AND CUTS —

the sun, dirt, and sand can irritate
it and slow down healing.

#448

REHYDRATE

dry hair after a day at the beach by spritzing on a leave-in conditioner, then blasting hair with a dryer.

great for ~~dry~~ *hair!*

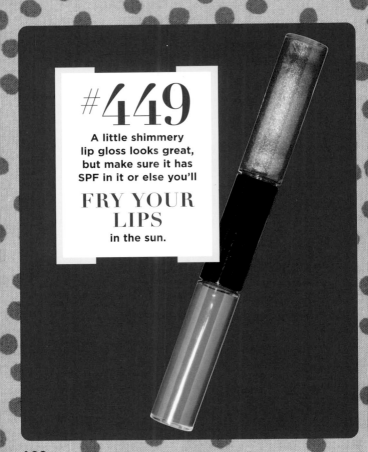

#449

A little shimmery
lip gloss looks great,
but make sure it has
SPF in it or else you'll

FRY YOUR
LIPS

in the sun.

#450

Get

INSTANT VOLUME

in humid weather by changing your part. Try a low side part or a zigzag one— it's an easy way to reenergize your style.

#451

SHIMMER
IN THE SUN

by sprinkling a
very fine loose gold
powder on your hair.

great for acne-prone skin!

#452

COVER BODY ACNE

with a long-lasting concealer before you go to the beach. Apply it *after* you put on sunscreen to prevent streaking.

#453

For a more

NATURAL LOOK,

skip foundation and use tinted moisturizer (with SPF) to even out your skin tone.

#454

Use bronzer on your eyelids instead of shadow to give them a warm color that

COMPLEMENTS YOUR TAN.

NEW

Neutrogena®

Fresh
Cooling

SUNBLOCK GEL

S P F
30

with
elioplex™
spectrum uva·uvb

NTLY COOLS
PROTECTS

RMATOLOGIST
ENDED SUNCARE

OZ (118 mL)

#455

SUN
EXPOSURE

makes scars and
hyperpigmentation more
noticeable. Wearing SPF 30
will help prevent this.

#456
NAVY LINER
will make the whites of your eyes sparkle and it's less harsh than black–perfect for hot weather months.

great for bronze skin!

#457

Try the

WET LOOK

at the beach. Smooth a
handful of conditioner
all over hair and pull it back.

Dove.

go fresh
THERAPY
conditioner

energize

fruit & lemongrass scent
for normal hair

FL.OZ.(355 mL)

VOLUME COUTURE BY FACTOR Mascara

#458

Waterproof mascara is great for swimming, but you'll need an

OIL-BASED REMOVER

to get it off.

#459

LET HAIR AIR-DRY

in the summer to prevent damage. Apply a light gel to damp hair and twist into a bun. Let it dry naturally for a tousled look.

#460

STORE LIP GLOSS

in a ziploc bag when you're at the beach and keep it next to an ice pack so it stays cool—moisture and heat will cause makeup to spoil quickly.

#461

HIDE BURNED LIPS

with a nude or pinky-beige tinted balm— it'll help heal the burn *and* neutralize redness.

great for red hair!

#462

When exposed to sun, redheads' color gets dull and flat more easily than other hues. To protect yours: apply leave-in conditioner—and

WEAR A HAT!

#463

**Even a tinge
of tan is**

SUN
DAMAGE,
**which can bring on
wrinkles, freckles,
and cancer.**

#464

Use

CREAM BLUSHES

and eyeshadows when you go swimming—
they won't come off, even in water.

#465

ADD INTENSITY

to eyes when you're tan—line *only* inner rims of top and bottom lids with a black waterproof liner.

#466

DETANGLE

wet hair with a wide-tooth comb. If you use a brush, you risk breaking strands.

#467

Before using spray self-tanner step into your shower then apply it. It'll work like an

AT-HOME TANNING BOOTH,

making cleanup easy.

Neutrogena®

MicroMist™ Tanning

SUNLESS SPRAY

DEEP

3 SHADES DARKER than your skin tone

AIRBRUSH
NO RUB APPLICATION

ultra-light, fine mist goes on evenly and works at any angle for an all-over flawless tan

NET WT 5.3 OZ (150 g)

#468

To

LIGHTEN BLONDE HAIR,

steep one chamomile tea bag in a cup of hot water. Let cool, spritz it on strands, and hit the beach.

#469

SCRUB

**before using
self-tanner, so
it's absorbed
more easily—
for even color.**

NEW

Neutrogena®

Ultra Sheer

DRY-TOUCH
SUNBLOCK

SPF
55

with
helioplex™
broad spectrum uva·uvb

**ULTRA LIGHT
CLEAN FEEL**

non-greasy, leave
soft and smo

**#1 DERMATOLO
RECOMMENDED SUNCAR**

3.0 FL OZ (88 mL)

#470

Put on sunblock
before applying
makeup, it will
give your skin a
healthy and

GLOSSY
DEWY.

#471

Mix a touch of

BRONZER

with a dab of sunblock to create a protective tinted lip balm.

#472

GET BEACHY WAVES

at the pool: put 1 tbsp. salt and 1 cup water in a spray bottle, then spritz the mixture on your hair.

#473

AVOID
SCALP
SUNBURN

by spritzing sunscreen
on your part and
along your hairline.

#474

Since too much sun exposure
can turn pale polishes
yellow or gray, apply a

SUN PROTECTING
TOP COAT

whenever you paint your
nails a light shade.

#475

PROTECT HAIR

from chlorine's drying effect. Apply conditioner to dry hair, make a ponytail, *then* swim.

great for
bronze/deep skin!

#476

Smudge

GREEN EYELINER

along top and bottom lashes to contrast with your warm skin tone.

#477
REALLY MOISTURIZE
your hair well by coating it with conditioner, then sitting in the sun for 10 minutes.

great for dry hair!

MATRIX

amplify
volumizing system

2 conditioner
revitalisant
acondicionador

CALIFORNIA BABY

SPF30+
SUNBLOCK STICK

Very Water
SPF3

no

F
Non-Ch
Tear
UVA-UVB Broa
no nut oils, g
For Babies,

50 c

#478

REAPPLY SPF 30

every two hours and
immediately after swimming.

#479

SHIELD YOUR COLOR

from the sun by spraying wet or dry hair every morning with a UV protective spray.

#480

To make your

SKIN GLOW,

use an aerosol-spray sunscreen— it will add a pretty sheen to your body *and* protect your skin.

great for
acne-prone skin!

#481

Wipe your face with cleansing pads every two hours (then reapply sunscreen) to

PREVENT ACNE.

#482

Shimmery, ultra
JUICY-LOOKING LIPS
are the perfect complement to bronze skin.

#483

Apply at least
2 OUNCES
(an entire shot glass),
or more of sunscreen
until your body is
completely covered up.

TABLESPOONS   OUN

— 2 TBSP.

— 1-1/2 TBSP.

— 1 TBSP.

— 1/2 TBSP.

#484

No need to wear full-on makeup when lounging in the sun. Instead,

APPLY BRONZER

to your cheeks, nose, and forehead for a sun-kissed look.

#485

In a pinch, use a little sunscreen instead of a styling product to TAME FRIZZIES.

#486

Start your day with a

NATURAL GLOW:

dab peach cream blush on your cheeks, then apply a nude SPF balm to protect your lips from the sun.

#487

BRAIDS
are a sexy and fuss-free way to wear hair poolside.

506

#488

WIPE OFF

your mascara wand
with a tissue before
applying it for the
most natural finish.

#489

WASH COTTON HATS

and visors after every two wears to
remove oil buildup that can cause
breakouts on your forehead.

#490

If you must use concealer, make sure you use a liquid form, it will look most natural in the heat since it's

NOT POWDERY.

#491

Neon-colored polishes like tangerine and

FUCHSIA

are the shades of summer. Wear one coat on nails and two coats on toes for a fun hit of color.

#492

PREVENT WRINKLES

before they start by wearing oversize
sunglasses to protect delicate skin around eyes.

great for
fair skin!

#493

Pair

SEAFOAM-
colored cream shadow
with sheer lips for a
girly, pool-side look.

#494

APPLY SUNSCREEN

even if you're wearing clothes! A white shirt provides protection only up to SPF 9; a black shirt; up to SPF 10.

#495

Avoid

INGROWN HAIRS

around your bikini line by swiping the area with a medicated pad that contains salicylic acid.

#496

A bright

STRAWBERRY COLORED

stain worn with a bare face is a hot (but natural!) look for summer.

great for
bronze / deep skin!

#497

Mix your moisturizer with foundation that is one shade darker than your skin for a subtle overall

BRONZE EFFECT.

#498

Try a bright, waterproof
eye pencil that

MATCHES YOUR
SWIMSUIT —

just keep the rest of
your face natural.

#499

USE A SCARF

or small sarong as a headband. Fold it up then wrap it around your head and ponytail and tie.

new

Nair ®

pretty

soft kiwi

hair remover
spray

Smooth Skin
that Lasts Longer

WITHOUT
cuts and
razor bumps

NET WT. 4.6 OZ (130g)

#500

SHAVE
your legs the
night before you
hit the beach so
the salt water
doesn't sting your
skin or irritate it.

index

photos

527